FROM NIGHTLIGHT S TO DAYBLOOMS

GAURAV KARKI

FROM NIGHTLIGHTS TO DAY BLOOMS

ISBN:-978-93-90994-26-7

ABOUT THE AUTHOR

Gaurav Karki, born in 2005, hails from Nainital, Uttarakhand, where he currently resides. He completed his early schooling at Sanwal School in Nainital and later enrolled at St. Joseph's College, Nainital, for his higher education.

At the age of 13, Gaurav discovered his passion for writing. Alongside his interest in plant spotting, he found solace in writing poetry. His creative endeavors are greatly influenced by the talented American singer-songwriter, Taylor Swift.

Prior to embarking on his solo debut work, Gaurav contributed to two anthologies. His latest book comprises a collection of poems that delve into various themes, including navigating through life and encountering the complex emotions as a queer individual and finding beauty in life's perplexing moments. From grappling with an identity crisis to pondering existential questions, this book encapsulates the writer's personal journey, growing up in a small town.

GAURAV KARKI

CONTENTS

WHAT IS PRIUN?

P: PUBLISHINGR:
ROOF
I: INCREDIBLE VERSEU:
UTMOST
N: NAVIGABLE

Priun Publication is not only a publication house but an idea to give platform to the authors who spend a lot of efforts on their content but do not get much royalty out of their books.

Priun Publication's founder Priyanka Sharma has a unique idea to set up the publication house with the help of people who were already in the field and have an idea to put the authors to their readers in a unique way. Readers always look for the flavor set to their mood and we ensure the readers get their flavor from us.

This publication house is dedicated to all such talents who want to put their talent to the readers directly from heart and be the rightful owner of their book. We have taken an oath to manage every author's expectations.

Writer's Note

Title: "From Nightlights to Dayblooms"

I chose the title "From Nightlights to Dayblooms" for my book because it reflects the recurring themes of the moon and flowers in the following poems. The moon has always been my source of inspiration, urging me to rise every time I face setbacks and driving me to write. Its various phases have taught me valuable lessons, both in darkness and brightness. Often described as "calm and composed," the moon has consistently soothed my anxiety, casting its faint light to guide me out of darkness and illuminate the right path.

"The moon brings an end to the somberness of the sky."

Flowers, as gifts from nature, hold the power to evoke memories of both joyful and challenging times through their fragrances.

But why do we experience anxiety? Why does sadness sometimes overshadow the possibility of happiness within our imagined worlds?

Our thoughts are influenced by the realities that surround us. We often create idealized versions of people in our minds, ignoring the fact that everyone, like the moon, has a dark side. Relationships, as described by many of my friends, are delicate and can crumble due to a single mistake. These poems draw inspiration from the peculiar emotions I have felt when the people I aspired to be with forever departed. These emotions are transformed into stories and tales that may seem fictional, but they reflect the depth of my involvement in these relationships. I crafted these tales to make my pain more relatable.

In my perspective, love encompasses not only the beautifully fragile bond between you and your partner but also the connections you share with your loved ones. Expressing me through writing has aided in understanding and sorting through my emotions. I created an "imperfect" character to represent a lover, someone flawed yet captivating. As you delve into the pages of this book, you will explore the expansive realm of love and relationships, accompanied by the anxiety that accompanies their potential collapse.

It's important to note that this book is not a work of fiction; it draws inspiration from real-life events and experiences. I wrote it as a means to navigate the suffocating "woods of anxiety" I found me in, and as a way to find solace and inner calm.

ACKNOWLEDGEMENTS

Special vote of thanks to:
My readers, for their love and support
Lord, who has always answered my prayers.
Jaya Chaudhary, my wonderful cousin for her support and guidance because of which I grew up as a writer,
My parents, sisters **Poornima**, **Kiran** and **Manasvi** for always helping me and supporting me.
Lastly, of the friends for their suggestions, support and showering me with unconditional love.

Credits: Gitanjali by Rabindranath Tagore, folklore, evermore by Taylor Swift, anonymous sources.

CHAPTER I.

Like Fallen leafs in September

FROM NIGHTLGHTS TO DAY BLOOMS

The falling:
Whispers of September

Dear September,

You're the remnants of the afterglow of all the crimson leaves on that trodden sidewalk; you're the scarlet crackles of the maple fireworks. You're the flannel shirt I like; you're like the liquor of nostalgia stirred into melancholy.

You're the bittersweet aftertaste on my tongue. You're the susurrus rustle of the oaks fiddling with the willow boughs. You're the harvest moon of my birth month. You're the gibbous drawn 'round my wounds that don't heal. You're the crescent in my crisis of faith. That scar that runs down your cheeks is like craters on the moon.

You're Saturn adorned with blue-aster-rings; you're the hand I hold as the aftermath of my broken home. I fidget with your fingers like a child, my head on your shoulder, and that breeze, oh September! Your fingers are my favorite fidgets. Your arms are my home, and your shoulder is the pillar that keeps me from falling.

You're my trust, so never let go of my hand, and let me adore your jasper eyes,

For in some,

I'll be wandering in a foreign land,

Where I won't be my own September,

And you'll reside in a world of dreams.

You flare upon the mountains of my hometown like the most beautiful daydream;

Let me be armed by your arms.

Your currents will always beckon my broken soul

'cause I'm half your reflection.

The root of writing:

A poet's muse

I want to share something with you,

I feel like I'm losing everyone

Every hand grows cold and time slips away,

Hours turn into months in the blink of an eye.

When I open my eyes after a monotonous day,

My time feels fragmented and washed away, as waves of overwhelming pain crash upon me.

Every grip becomes sweaty, every face fades,

Transforming into mere lines in the stories I write.

The memories turn into empty voids, devoid of the stardust that once filled them.

It's terrifying to dream of stars,

Knowing they may bring destructive meteors, causing cataclysms in my universe.

But still, I dream of starlight, because I am a raconteur.

I weave tales that bring light and brilliance,

But they fade into the dimness of moonless nights.

My words are like tides,

Rising with the full moon, falling with the new,

Never constant, always shifting and drifting like ether.

I have some questions I want to ask,

Have I lost you? I don't know.

My intuition, for once, I hope is false and unfounded.

This may be my last chance,

My subconscious mind plays tricks on me, which I do not speak of.

I have felt like I've died many times,

My words now sink into silence,

Like withered blooms on barren winter lands.

My birch has burnt down to ashes, submerged in this desolation.

Yet, I hold on to the belief,

Like the waxing crescent moon blooming eternally,

That there is a rhythm in this gentle melody,

That will guide me through the darkness.

Within the depths of my inner self,

Where the perilous cliffs of pain reside,

Pushing me into years of darkness,

Your answers will become my guiding light.

These faces may be confined to grainy, distorted pictures,

But your touch will never fade away.

You will stay with me, with your hand preventing me from falling into the abyss.

Loving you was never a crime, my muse.

Of lovers and longing:

The evening by the sea

They say poetry is transcendental.

So, I sat by the placid shore on a cold Thursday evening. The waves echoed back at the midnight sea, swiftly sweeping the sand, all hushed as haunted.

Everything's so still, yet my empty eyes speak.

The moon spills celestial liquor all over my skin, with an ache of eternal longing, no one but you know the pain I bear as words transcend down the scars of my being.

These hands want to be held in a pale knot of your strength.

I look for you, Augustus, the king of my heart, when July shares gentle kisses with the moon-blanched muddy bed and the rain-soaked winds, everything's serene, yet the air sings elegies for you, you are gone. Yet another faint midnight, the parched earth soaks itself in the rain of anguish, and the cracks and crevices flood with water. The trembling waves fill every eye with horror yet my core stays from crumbling against an invincible disaster - of our colliding hearts.

Yes, our eyes don't meet, if they do, our hearts collide too, my beloved. The moon shrieks its scars in the lonely sky, with you being its sole aid. And I can't bear another apocalypse, when the dusk comes to me in the loveliest shades of blue, because stolen stares tell lies.

Only lies.

Thoughts and contemplations: That evening in my hometown

I love my hometown.

The distant hills, on which the sun gleams, beckon me every faint afternoon. I'm sitting on my balcony, watching the mundane day fade.

The serenity of the birds melts away the dread of the season. Yet, my heart sinks. The question pounds my head.

Why does everything have an inevitable end?

The undulating hills, the panoramic pastures, and golden meadows, the oak, fir, and spruce, the playful fiddle of the jays and the sparrows. The hushed murmurs of the rustling oaks and the swirling clouds, too, gradually dwindle.

My fear, too, will eventually die out.

But the time we had together, too, comes to an end.

It turns out to be my worst nightmare.

My sister once told me,

"There's no end to materialism."

And so, I find my solace in the gurgling brooks and the flowers. They, too, exude exuberance.

My mind mingles with them.

I find happiness in the Earth's creation.

Things that are alive are beautiful.

They gradually come to an end, and so, my most beloved,

I could be in your arms and lie there until my skeleton collapses.

I want to be loved like a little child.

I want to be loved in all innocence.

I want to fall asleep in your arms, forgetting all my worldly fears. I want to meld into your arms. I want to collide with your bones. Bleed into you.

Fall into the eternal sleep of death,

And meet me where the lilies bloom and souls coincide.

Let them twine with my collarbones,

Dwell in my empty gaze of eternity.

That day, I would truly rest in peace.

Wandering ourselves astray: The Lighthouse

I sit in the corner,

Reading in dim light

About sad tales and bad sights

Exhausted,

You draw the curtains,

Catch a dreamy foreground,

Staring at the ships which roll down

The old harbour,

As the fog deepens

I had heard the sea shore sounds like seagulls.

Right at midnight,

I watch the moonrise with tired eyes, with one around, except for you.

When I find myself amid the town draped in perfect silence

Staring at the placid sea

The entire town asleep,

Only you and I, still wide awake, listening to honking of the horns of the distant ships, attending the waves as they crash on the shore.

I wonder if we could dwell in the lighthouse atop the steep cliffs,

Shining crystal jets on the dark waters, so as they radiate.

Stay up all night.

To show paths to the midnight cruises, harkening the sea's everlasting music.

Conjunction of Eyes: When heaven witnessed our love

Fate knows what he has chosen for us, but even in the universe, which lies tangential to ours,

I would always choose you.

We would sit beneath the stars, talk to the moon.

In that brief moment of illumination, we would be ourselves,

Free and safe from the bounds of the world that has always haunted me,

Most beloved,

And the heavens would melt to become havens when they witness the conjunction of our eyes.

Our worlds seem to melt when our hands part, and these people have the audacity to ask if it would be hard to bid farewell.

This is the ode to the same hands that have caressed my naked soul, that have planted love on my bare body. On painful nights, I dream of your gentle hands on my scars.

And I wonder,

"How do I say goodbye?"

Whispers and Havens: the night he held me

He knows all my whispers and murmurs, and all which haunts my existence

-the terrible garden of thoughts with mouldered walls, broken fences, and ivy that's scattered all over it, flowers of frozen gestures and torn letters-all that is feared by me.

I'm scared of dullness and wreckage, but I find dreadful peace in storms-in all that's dead and dying, wilted moss-memoirs, and fierce waves of hurt, because he rises above it all, the misery of my broken and haunted existence, my downtrodden self and my broken image.

I find my haven in his arms, the fingers having crossed mine made my world thrive and burgeon, the hands which have held my bones and soul in them,

The hands I've shared clovers with.

Chapter II.

Spring, the scent of winter and the impending storm

Springs fragrance: a closet full of flowers and butterflies

These wildflowers graze my soul with subtle vibrancy.

The chamomiles in the closet,

The delusional daisies,

The halcyon hyacinths,

The fleeting fuchsia

Listless lilacs

Adorn my skull, wrenching me with heart-stopping hues.

Suspended in their petals, within me,

It's the complexion of dusk in thc woods by the shoreline.

A fleet of vehement sensations, closeted in my skull, hovers over my head.

The seashore suspiring the salt air, settled in perfect ambiance,

As if it was "the archetype of the seaside at dusk break."

The twilit waves crash on the

Crepuscular shore,

Stirring a song of melancholia in my bones,

While I let your lips taste my soul.

Time will whirl in its cosmic routine,

But I stay there with the cessation of seconds,

While at the coast,

I boast to the sea, for an eternity, about my lover.

Sea sorrow

A rover with a melancholy soul

Unwinding ties with the cynical fouls

Unsettled,

Unnerved,

Relentless and

Restless

Suspiring the salt air of the western Coast cape.

Bliss seems delusional

And suffering ceaseless

When you hear her sorrowful wail

Reverberating far as 100 yards

From the great sea

With them oblivion of her despair

What did they do?

What did she suffer?

With the night sky being somber and starless.

The soulful melody of the sea waves crashing the steep shore were the only ways of her catharsis.

But they made her have an epiphany of her died grace.

And everything faded with time,

Now she lays supine in her grave.

Now that the smoke chokes you and you can't breathe,

You realized her presence made your monotony of captivity in these confined walls idyllic.

Your Arms Bear the Warmth Of A Cardigan

I hum the tone underneath my breath,

The same tone that crawls over my skin.

And then runs deeper in

Some say I try to mask my pain behind metaphors “drastically overdramatic”,

But that's a well laid plot.

I blocked the world out behind the door shutting it close.

There are you who I want to be with.

Though you're a universe away,

We still gaze at the same stars.

We spend our days the same ways,

Under the spotlight of cross examination,

The days tinted of monochrome.

My lacustrine sorrow surges when I sit at the verge of the placid twilit waters.

I've spoilt them from my tears and their dusky tone blends with the nightfall,

The dusk has embedded itself in me.

My soul is growing caliginous.

My hope succumbs to these dark clouds eclipsing the welkin.

The red gate of what I thought to be paradise will unroll again, this time, with my ecstasy growing old.

But there's a only one chance of wildflowers sprouting from my barren body and blooming

-you wrapping me in your cardigan arms, pulling me out of this listless trance,

Making me dream of unfading rainbows.

Catastrophe

I can see myself crash to the floor.

My nostrils are blowing smoke and my chest feels heavy and burning, as if it was a hearth. My sun is drowning in the somber clouds that are looking over my city that wants to see the winter sun, but it's cold and pelted away by a hailstorm.

It all sits still until midnight.

I sit in the balcony until the clock strikes one. The moon catches fire and burn down to ashes and the sky turns dark once again. I put down the enameled tea cup on the wooden table until it starts to spill all over.

The hands of the clock tower are melting away with the aurora, they trickle until they wreck the cobblestones breaking down the golden bridges submerging them ten feet down the barren ground. A downpour of thoughts leads to a breakout of tears, on my drought stricken barren mind, with shallow breaths filling my hollows. The city siren blows loudly until my ears hurt. I pull the drawer to get some cinnamon for my sore throat that's aching from last night's catastrophe.

Withering bones,

Wilting souls

I wonder if it's a fever dream.

I let my sadness eulogize me.

A graveyard painted with literal skulls flowers and butterflies.

'til they flood my head, metaphors.

Someone told me "Stop doing cliffhanging in the name of metaphors" But the impact that my skull inundated by memoirs inscribes and embeds the ink in ways that unearth the buried scars from their grave

Every time the words are uttered.

But what are the best metaphors?

"Poets bloom from their muses"

Yes, I Bloom because of you. You are my essence and I'm rooted firmly to your ground.

Your love still makes me dizzy

From the butterflies in my stomach

If your love made me bloom, then this separation has witheredme.

I'm lying in the grave of veracity. If the greys are suspended in the air, you suddenly turn them blue.

Does that make me happy?

I don't know. Spring is breaking loose, pulling all the clovers out from the bare earth.

But,

I cannot bloom. I Bloom once in a lifetime

I bloom because of you.

You may raconteur, you tell many tales.

But what I never want to hear from you

Is that you never loved me.

CHAPTER III:

The wildest winter

<u>Fetching prose, taming my grief.</u>

What do my poems imply when they're flooded with one plain emotion—grief?

Grief and I are synonymous. I create grief in the most artistic ways, picking the most peculiar shades to craft my prose.

From the wilting flowers and the thunderclouds rolling over grey skies, I don't choose the calmness of the moon leaving its cloudy cradle. Grief is the cause of artistry.

Where do I fetch my grief from? Where do I get my greys from?

Do I get them from the dark waters cascading *down* my distant vision of the dusky ravine? Or from watching the grave of my fretful contemplations unfurl into shades of red, orange, and blue?

But what if I tell you it's none?

Muses are beautiful people, and so was mine. But what if I tell you that my muse broke my heart? It was the day melancholy became a permanent resident of my core.

Yet,

I'm habitual in sowing shades of grief in the wasteland of my decaying body, harvesting reaps of prose I water with my invincible tears for the sake of catharsis.

The Tragedy of the broken moon

There

was

no

p a r a ll e l

to

the

moon,

But so many to me.

2) I was trying to make the best out of my ruins,

But now I'm only left with

"Isn't the moon so pretty?"

Tucked somewhere underneath my tongue, ready to be rolled out, but it dies.

3) Silence inflicts itself upon my lips as a grave illness. It rots in my lips into a lifeless frame.

4) I know you won't run back into these longing arms of mine,

Aren't waves always supposed to meet the shore?

5) I eyed upon you like you were the moon.

But you now hate the moon because I told you it wasn't as pretty se you, it reminds you of how your drunken lips kissed my cheeks, and all of a sudden, it was June.

6) It has been thirteen years. I'm still in the classroom haunted by memorics, and darkness has inhabited the spot where you left me. The illusion broke, but it's still gloomy now.

7) My anxiety paralyzes me. I look at the disoriented world through a cold blue filter, which the moon's disintegrated pieces have set. I look at myself in the mirror, but my figure is a skeleton. All I see is a skull clumsily fixed over a bony neck, with ribs ejecting from the corners.

The mirror screams in pain from such disintegration as I fall to the ground in chaos, as my ability to think cripples to unthinkable.

Heeding Hollows

Something seemed grand but was hollow,

Our love,

You dropped my heart of glass.

You conspired to scar me, but you scarred your crumbling soul.

A red rose froze on the cold ground.

Trapped,

Wading in circles, the repetitive melancholia renews with each whirl of the clock. Its tarnished hands move interruptedly, with halts. A somber tone settles in my soul slowly, dispersing and dissipating in wisps.

"I feel melancholic and grey today," I say,

But then,

A hush descends upon my throat,

The silence seals my lips.

I shouldn't have censored the red lights.

The luxurious fancy hotel in the grand east estate,

Sitting in the filamentous light obscured by the curtains,

I wonder, gin-soaked from vinous musings, interrupted by the infringement of quietude.

The day rewinds,

The rustling winds, the clock tower, the loud screeches of cars rushing down the main road. I stand in the corner, in the shade of the store's awning, wondering how it all went wrong.

I remember when our fingers brushed while keeping our hands on the doorknobs.

The vines hanging from the store's stone walls remind me of how you used to rest your head on my shoulder at 7 pm while at the theatre.

We walked out, and now I'm alone at our old spot, and your seat is empty.

A squall brings in a thunderstorm at the door. The

windows clank from the violent thunder.

My mind floods with bitter nostalgia that crashes with the shore of my brittle soul.

The greyness of the sky coalesces in my bones.

I gave you all of my love, but all you gave me was hurt.

Honey, all you gave me was hurt, gave me fake niceties.

It still hurts in my bones, from falling for you.

Listener

I want to tell you something tonight,

Sometimes I just don't feel proud of myself,

My infectious throat fills with shallow breaths while I sit on the couch,

Punching the typewriter keys,

That's when I want you to hold me, I'm crumbling.

You hear me breathe.

But then I can't capture this feeling as it drags me into darkness. Can't you see?

All you hear is just the heaviness of the breaths.

I try to dissolve this numbing in my chest as I gulp down the evening tea.

There's no one to hear the screams I never shouted,

The only difference in my place,

The ambience is not serene.

The roof drips dreariness on me,

I can't sleep.

Honey, I can't sleep.

When these melancholic walls leak monotone, what reverberates in these walls, the floor's cacophonic creak,

Honey, you have no idea I can't speak,

When there's chafe in this cafe,

Will you dance with my soul?

Dance off my monotone,

While my eyes clatter and begin to perish with this ferocious war that's raging in me,

Honey,

Can you hear me?

You know there's more than bruises and blood, past this nightfall,

Though my cosmos succumbed to the voids,

My moon has burnt down to ashes.

I gave you my time, my love, my mind.

All you did to me was leave, and now I'm dying.

When I'll not have the courage to hold my sword and the good time will be biting the dust in cloaks of blood,

Will you tend my soul snapped right in two?

Will you not be a silent bystander of the street?

Will you hear me when no one else will?

Honey,

When you can't hear me now, how will you,

When I'll bleed to death from your haunting smirk?

Now that I'm addressing you over and over again,

Will you figure out I need you?

Will you hear me?

Now that I'm arguing that you'll not leave,

There will be happiness in me,

While I stand here watching the languid sea.

Will you hear me?

Spineless

I've been thrown out many times, until I stepped out on my own.

Was I not allowed to?

Then why do you ask, if my head hurts from flaring pictures of pain over the phone's screen?

Hurt,

Swirling in my chest,

Dripping from my eyes,

Spilling over the counter,

Crashing to the bedroom floor.

I've been so sad,

As if I've seen

The last moon.

From all the days I've spent

Staring at the rippling iridescence of the moon

In muddy pools on a full moon day:

The solace to the scars you've given me,

As they turn into eulogies of feverish dreams.

I look, I hope, I dream of being found

In my non-existentialism.

I've melded into chaos

In mending my collapsing self.

You were the solace to me,

The blues of my heart.

You know what I mean.

But then you tore me apart.

I melt from this toxicity,

As the moon wanes into a void,

Long before I even see another crescent.

Spineless,

ever-changing,

Just unlike you said.

I melt into my grave,

Long before your goodbye.

Dying,

Pressed in the corner,

Unnoticed like a wallflower,

With a new poem rotting in my bones.

Gave you love as no one could,

But you left me like an

Open wound.

But I don’t want to be a scar to your being,

And hence, I leave.

But you’ll miss me,

Won’t you?

Disembodiment

And sometimes when I close my eyes,

I see the woods painted on my eyelids

As if they were a blank canvas

With dark, masked figures crawling deeper into me,

Making their way inside, and it feels lethal.

Like a Cavern, I feel hollow

And it seems that I'm imaginative but eerie

With psychotic screams filling me

Echoing at the deepest end,

I'm shaking,

Shivering

Trembling,

Stumbling

And falling

And at the deep end, it's nothing, but hollowness

And in the hollowness, it's only peculiarity.

It's filling me with insecurities

You know I bought lavender seeds from mine euphoria, to plant in yours

~~The seeds plucked out of the sanitized hands pricked at the nail ends~~

Seeds of cappella burrowed from rain

And you dressed to gift them in a giveaway of attention, unapologetically.

And sometimes I feel like my skin is sinking into my bones, deeper and further

And I will be nothing but bones

And vines will creep from the hollows and crevices

Of my skull and ribs adorning me with flowers

Will then my grave be marked as holy?

The Anatomy of a Wasteland Patch

I sit in the front porch shade,

Sipping sweet summer tea.

Five feet away from my dwelling lays virgin wasteland patch,

A pasture crammed with a Linnet's cry.

I recall,

It stood still beneath the sky

Saturated with the moon glistening all over it,

Sited in stillness.

Until you came and trampled upon all the wildflowers.

They die until the next summer,

When they rise from the dead ground

With their worn-down souls dissolved in melancholic elegies.

They somehow blink at me and they bear your smile.

I cull one before they submerge you in your deathbed

It's still in my drawer,

Bearing the scent of my loss.

The air that bears its perfume makes me have an epiphany,

~~All of you contained in its smell~~.

It longs for your virgin touch

The others are toxic they have absorbed your skin; their roots are tangled with your bones.

I pull one hard but they have an affinity for your cold skeleton.

The roots of toxicity are ingrained in your thoughts.

I embrace you with sweaty hands, but you slip away from my grip.

You know you'll be yourself only when the illusion breaks

There's no cure but prayers for an ailment as a broken heart.

The Café

Monotony hangs from my lips while I sit in the cafe chattering over your face. The front porch inviting me from days, as a fleet of holiday's flings over my head, there's on one plain feeling in me, of stodgy evenings. The cool chats while sauntering down paved pathways past parking lots seem unfamiliar to me, for some reason I trudge up the same streets. The table cloth, the scented candles at the dinner shop,

Just everything reminds me of your cold touch on typical winter evenings.

The vintage days of unspoken vows, my time-worn prose's acquiring bouquet as of aged wine. A monochrome Polaroid with a folded smile pressed within the walls of a leather wallet, us sipping tea in the rain, while we sat in the front porch light, from witnessing a love songs debut on the vintage radio, to all of the gift-wrapped vinyl and vintage stereos. A truant glance, an awkward grin,

When a static stare pauses the moment

It stops in time but it won't stay forever, like it will fade away into bareness in which the voices in my head tremble and shake It's like we've known each other for the longest of time. But then,

You leave

The traces are clear

The vague stammers I utter subconsciously.

A language you could hear and I could speak.

Your hug bears the warmth to melt my frigid heart on a numbing day,

But then my words turned into cliché

And now I sit in the corner, haunted by the dim light and skeptical talks of folks that were aphonic onlookers of the silent street.
They now speak out loud,

Their agonizing words make me bleed.

<u>A eulogy to broken May</u>

May is such a broken month; I can see the cracks already

And hear

The clank of my heart breaking into few more million pieces

May is so wrecked yet it floods,

The bare earth with a million weeds but the flowers die,

The hearts heal of cracks but with un-weary heartaches,

Faces flooding with smiles, while the soul has snapped right into two,

And amidst this wreckage I'm not sure if one more poem dies inside of me.

It is the similar haze that blinds me, the monsoons drenching the noon wet, drowning the moon in fluffy greys, painting the sky with a moon halo.

I wonder if beauty hints at the impending storm to which spring will succumb,

To which spring yearns for a warm blister but the rain has already ruined it.

The poets have died at such a sight,

and so have their muses.

My heart has worn down to fragments to the impending heartache of lost spring,

An unforgettable moment of lost love inflicts itself as unmitigated moments of pain

As I watch the Lilacs parched on the garden's wall.

Spring lies somewhere in between of leaving and dying, with weeds inundating it, and flocks of zephyr lilies,

I'm consumed by them;
they're reminiscent of a past mostly ugly, but their fragrance brings the very essence of me, my innocence.

My frail heart builds walls of prose

Against an otherwise invincible cataclysm,

With fragrance of the flowers until spring,

But it hangs somewhere between collapsing, breaking and crumbling, as my verses grow darker.

You were enough darling,

But now I'm dying just from the war between you and me,

We never speak.

And I yearn for you and spring.

And May's so broken,

I can already see the cracks.

Caliginous Crepuscule

The blues are bound to cast a spell.

I wade out in the countryside at the hours when the incandescence of the last sun rays begins to blend with the gloaming, ready to set the twilit night.

At the downtown mansion, the willow branches hang from the moldering walls standing on a plot of dry land, submerging within the caliginosity of crepuscule at the dying summer hours. The neatly pleated tablecloth and the wilted flowers lay there unmarred in a static condition.

My weary feet ache, but they want to dance with the hallucinations

To the song my wine-soused lips utter.

The same song saturates the trenches, then sublimates in wisps.

The fragile blooms sneak in subtly from the earth, and they watch, bewildered.

The panorama painted with the twilit lunatic glow has the power to make me want to balter, but this infatuation of mine has smothered my flames.

I'm left with nostrils blowing ashes,

But I don't want to set all my skin on fire one more time.

I dreamt of fertility in futility, of fidelity.

I want to thrive,

I want to swing amongst this thicket of darkling birches again,

For the ivy in me hasn't withered yet.

It never will.

Chapter IV:

Next summer

Midsummer's evening

Its summer and the city lights are fading into oblivion. The azure breaks into a vibrant violet and spectacular turquoise with a pink gradient, just as I watch the deliquescent eve evanesce into night.

The colours are scattered along the bridge leaving their trails, the sun fades, stars draw themselves on the sky's arch and the planets dangle from the eaves. The great river flows in shades of lavender-cherry, the reflection of the sickle moon ripples upon the twilit waters as I run my fingers in a playful fiddle, bespeckling me instinctively with the colours of the night.

The night deepens, I feel summer's warm embrace on my skin, in the city's concrete lap.

It envelopes all of me, till I've felt every breath of mine pass with time,

It's when I've felt alive, truly alive.

Gumusservi

I walked down the town lanes one evening when the distant industrial chimney was exploding smoke into the crystal air.

It blew until evening, until they smothered the fire. The thick black smoke slowly rose up, choking me, so I flew towards the woods, meandering, feeling elated, as I baltered from the serenity. Until I saw the moon-brooch, warning me of an approaching storm in a whimsical tone, with the orphic feeling inscribed in my bones.

My plastic ribs protected my heart of glass. I soaked my feet in cliffside pools, with the whirling water dissolving my grief. Counting my scars with each breath, my time was shuffled like an hourglass turned again and again.

My kalopsia made the gumusservi balter over the lake, with the lullaby lingering at the periphery of my thoughts or the songs I whispered under my breath. It was so calm to sit beneath the stars and sing out elegies to the moon.

Unraveling the Sadness Within:

Self embrace

Vulnerability seems foreign to those who don't appear to be crumbling. Your own insecurities make you feel on the verge of strangeness, rarity at its peak. The same people compare me with the lake poets, while I call them overly obsessive, overdramatic, and manic, drawn to a delusional world. Some advocate for grounding oneself in reality and staying away from delusions, justifying it as healthy to be rooted. But is it healthy to be rooted in sorrow?

None but sorrow seems to make sense in my physical existence.

There's catharsis in this hurt.

The scented waxen wisteria elicits fragrance to assuage my threadbare scars while I stand here.

Weren't the lake poets romantic like me?

But I, marred by scars of insurmountable hurt buried underneath my bruised skin and beaten veins, am different.

The sorrow in the marrow of my bones makes my soul downcast, yet painting me as romantic; I cherish it from my heart because winsomeness is nature's essence.

You fade into the barrenness of the drought in me and then flood my vulnerable end. But it will never overflow from these abyssal ribs, the fissures growing deeper and deeper.

The extremely ecstatic blues once bloomed there, but then the rain drenched them glossy, dissolving their perfume, their petals transmuting to slime, flooding my entire frozen ground. The submerged land filled with deceased blooms from the dead spring. The heady harmonies trapped in the chains of cacophonous noises from firm disbelief and utter nuisance.

These are the repercussions of long periods of despondency and ignorance.

I bury my words under my deceased tongue; you wonder who muted the lips that seemingly chattered every single minute. It's hard for you to believe, as if you don't see the cliffs in me and pools of insurmountable sadness. And you were successful in cutting ties with me, but no one will love you like I did.

This will haunt you forever because these skeptics never saw a love as pure as mine.

And I've embraced myself with the utmost euphoria.

These people will never understand the sadness in me, and hence, my beauty.

The empty dance of death

Sometimes, my heart feels empty, yet overflowing with longing.

It's a sort of feeling I'm yet to understand,

A thought that is yet to dawn upon me,

Awakenings and rebirth,

Yet I feel like I've lived enough.

It seems like it has been only a while basking in a field of sunflowers, and when I think I've danced enough, when all the flowers begin to shrivel and fall upon the parched ground the very next moment, and they take a moment, when they are reborn.

It's watching the cycle of life complete a full round.

It's a moment of beauty, of mysterious pondering.

Isn't death graceful?

Isn’t death important for creation?

Isn't the moon that hangs in the sky dead and graceful, isn't the sky nothing but a graveyard of our ancestors? Isn't it that every wing of a dead butterfly is kept?

Its winter at its peak, those everlastings have died,

But,

Have they lost their beauty?

If yes, then why do you keep them close to your heart?

Aren't I but born from poets long dead?

I guess there's a different grace in death.

Vincent's Yellow

I've been consuming sunflowers,

One at a time, for the snaps in the heart, the cracks in the soul, for the mouldering ribs and eyes exhausted from sorrow, to disguise my flawed self. Yet I cloak it with my sorrowful delirium, while the others die from the toxicity of an array of illusions.

Why only a yellow aid for a head that flares,

Musings like a melancholy kaleidoscope? They say Vincent van Gogh ate yellow to aid his sorrow, but he was considered insane, for the paint was toxic.

In the hope of painting himself yellow, he created beloved sunflowers.

Consuming the toxicity bit by bit, he found the beauty in himself through his art.

And so am I here, following him, surviving an existential crisis.

Melancholy with frenzy shrouds the scars from the war of words and silence. The mind and heart are on the verge of collapsing, from the absolute wreck of pseudo-happiness that fades away, being consumed by time.

What remains are the sunflowers!

And I,

Forever...

Moon-Child

It all starts with one glance at the moon.

When noon wears down to night,

All it does is languid lingering in the viridity of my naïve eyes.

It hovers over the clouds, until its glow is shattered over the bare earth.

With the fall of the first snow,

The delphiniums sprout out.

They soak up the poison shoved down their cups,

The acid their roots have absorbed.

But they'll swell with fragrance,

For they are the Moon's children!

They are sublime and fresh!

They surge up the waves, but then

The tide falls.

My words die out and rise up with the moon changing phases turbulently every night.

I'll sit here

Until I lose track of the pain I've kept in these days.

The lunar gleam dissolves the toxicity

And the futile blooms that float around in floodwater after the cataclysmic flood following a season of barren cold.

But after it settles, joy will reside here

In my heart,

And they'll bloom once again,

The moonflowers,

Forever after!

www.ingramcontent.com/pod-product-compliance
Lightning Source LLC
LaVergne TN
LVHW090126160826
845673LV00015B/1035
* 9 7 8 9 3 9 0 9 9 4 2 6 7 *